D1316865

MY KNEECAP SEEMS TOO LOOSE

365 random thoughts to inspire deeply shallow thinking

ronald p. culberson

GB
Gilbert Belle
Press

Gilbert Belle Press
Herndon, Virginia

My Kneecap Seems Too Loose
365 Random Thoughts to Inspire Deeply Shallow Thinking

Copyright © 2010 by Ronald P. Culberson

Published by Gilbert Belle Press, Herndon, VA in association with Central Plains Book, Arkansas City, KS.

Cover Design by Dunn + Associates Design
Author Photo by Frasier Photography
Text design by Ad Graphics, Inc.

Printed in the United States of America

ISBN: 978-0-9754077-1-4

For ordering information visit www.FUNsulting.com.

Dedication

This book is dedicated to my fellow
(in a general, non-sexist way) humorists.
I admire you more than you know.

Acknowledgements

I want to thank my good friend and business partner David Glickman who supported me from the start of this project although I'm sure he will deny any connection to the book if it is a big flop. He also gave me valuable feedback on what was funny and what was not. I did not use his feedback but I am grateful that he took the time to read the draft.

I also appreciate my humor writing recovery group members: Dale Irvin, Molly Cox, and Bill Stainton. Dale's help in changing the focus of the book was brilliant. Molly and Bill were cheerleaders from the start. But basically, none of them did any significant work on the book.

Dena Harris has been a faithful writing buddy since we met at the Erma Bombeck Writer's Workshop. We share a love for humor but not a love for cats. Of course, cats *are* funny, in an annoying kind of way. Dena gave me valuable advice on ellipses, commas, and when I might should have used the past pluperfect subjunctive tense. So, if there are grammatical errors in the book, I'd look to her for an explanation.

Almost lastly, I offer an acknowledgement that it is overlooked by most authors. I could not have written one sentence of this book had it not been for my Lenovo T61 laptop computer. Although it often suggested alternate spellings, it never failed to record exactly what I typed. I am deeply indebted and terribly sorry for the coffee spill on February 7, 2010, the day we lost ALT.

Finally, I thank my readers for having the faith or perhaps the blind ignorance to buy this book. It won't change your life but, if enough of you buy it, it could change mine. For that, I'm potentially grateful.

Introduction

This book began when I realized I was wasting good creative energy on daily random social media updates. Instead of putting them out for free, I decided to compile them in a book and make $12.95 on each copy sold.

And now, you too can create your very own random thoughts by using my deeply shallow thinking as inspiration. I suggest you follow these steps for getting the most out of this book:

1. Read one random thought every day.

2. Throughout the day, record your own thoughts in the space provided.

3. Chuckle at your cleverness.

4. Use your thoughts as social media updates, emails to friends, and voicemail messages.

5. Pick the best thought for your tombstone. Consider having it carved in advance as family members do not always appreciate cleverness during times of grief.

6. Tell everyone how random thoughts dramatically changed your thinking.

7. Before you die, encourage all of your friends to buy a copy of this book.

It's not rocket science.

MY KNEECAP SEEMS TOO LOOSE

365 random thoughts to
inspire deeply shallow thinking

It would be nice to have the ability to send an electric current through the phone when telemarketers call. Then I could say, "I'm shocked that you called me during dinner."

Your Random Thoughts:

_____

_____

_____

_____

_____

_____

I can't figure out why some Sudoku's are harder than others. They all use the same numbers.

Your Random Thoughts:

_____

_____

_____

_____

_____

_____

I'D LIKE TO SEE AN AUCTIONEER WALK THE TALK.

Your Random Thoughts:

_____

_____

_____

_____

_____

_____

If I daydream long enough, someone naked always appears.

Your Random Thoughts:

_____

_____

_____

_____

_____

_____

I just saw a photo of myself. I didn't look nearly as good as I do in the mirror.

Your Random Thoughts:

_____

_____

_____

_____

_____

_____

It's curious to me that swallowing saliva is normal but swallowing spit is disgusting.

Your Random Thoughts:

_____

_____

_____

_____

_____

_____

When I'm talking to someone, I never know what to do with my hands. Once I start thinking about them, they feel very big.

Your Random Thoughts:

_____

_____

_____

_____

_____

_____

One hole on my belt is too loose but the next one is too tight. Clearly, my waist is not standard size.

Your Random Thoughts:

_____

_____

_____

_____

_____

_____

Ever since I bought a computer, my handwriting has gotten progressively worse. Thank goodness my typimg is still goid.

Your Random Thoughts:

_____

_____

_____

_____

_____

_____

I love *USA Today* newspaper. The words are not real big and there aren't too many of them.

Your Random Thoughts:

_____

_____

_____

_____

_____

_____

Cats are arrogant. Even though I know I'm more talented, it still irritates me.

Your Random Thoughts:

_____

_____

_____

_____

_____

_____

Most people must look good to themselves. And that sure explains what they're wearing.

Your Random Thoughts:

_____

_____

_____

_____

_____

_____

If I say the word "weird" over and over, it sounds weird.

Your Random Thoughts:

_____

_____

_____

_____

_____

_____

There are certain clothes I have never found a reason to wear. Bathrobes, cowboy hats, cardigan sweaters, and thongs. And I would never wear them at the same time.

Your Random Thoughts:

_____

_____

_____

_____

_____

_____

Thinking is the enemy of sleep. But when I try to stop thinking, so I can get to sleep, thinking is all I can think about.

Your Random Thoughts:

_____

_____

_____

_____

_____

_____

There are only
eight musical notes.
With such limited
options, how can there
be new music after
all these years?

Your Random Thoughts:

_____

_____

_____

_____

_____

_____

When I try to listen to music *and* do something else, the two, baby, baby, get mixed up.

Your Random Thoughts:

_____

_____

_____

_____

_____

_____

The words "Las Vegas" sound like "lost wages." I don't think that's a coincidence.

Your Random Thoughts:

_____

_____

_____

_____

_____

_____

I'm never drawn to the books with a shirtless man on the cover.

Your Random Thoughts:

_____

_____

_____

_____

_____

_____

Sometimes the words "paper or plastic" just pop into my head.

Your Random Thoughts:

_____

_____

_____

_____

_____

_____

Best I can tell, ugly men are usually the ones who wear a toupee. So, it really doesn't improve the situation that much.

Your Random Thoughts:

_____

_____

_____

_____

_____

_____

I wonder if there are grief support groups for people who lost their keys?

Your Random Thoughts:

_____

_____

_____

_____

_____

_____

The sound of a dentist drill is one of the few sounds that hurts.

Your Random Thoughts:

_____

_____

_____

_____

_____

_____

I'm thinking of a number between 1 and 100. No, that's not it.

Your Random Thoughts:

_____

_____

_____

_____

_____

_____

Reading glasses make it much easier to see how old I look wearing reading glasses.

Your Random Thoughts:

_____

_____

_____

_____

_____

_____

I see men wearing both suspenders and a belt. Their pants must be very heavy.

Your Random Thoughts:

_____

_____

_____

_____

_____

_____

I THINK POETS ARE JUST LAZY WRITERS.

Your Random Thoughts:

_____

_____

_____

_____

_____

_____

The bad taste of Brussels sprouts does not surface until right before you swallow. By then, you're already committed.

Your Random Thoughts:

_____

_____

_____

_____

_____

_____

As old as the Rolling Stones are, they appear to have gathered no moss.

Your Random Thoughts:

_____

_____

_____

_____

_____

_____

There is a connection in my brain that forces me to push a door that says "Pull."

Your Random Thoughts:

_____

_____

_____

_____

_____

_____

I hate to get caught in the rain but I love to take a shower.

Your Random Thoughts:

_____

_____

_____

_____

_____

_____

When it comes to "ready, set, go," I believe that once we're ready, we should be allowed to go.

Your Random Thoughts:

_____

_____

_____

_____

_____

_____

IT WOULD BE IRONIC IF A BOXER WORE BRIEFS.

Your Random Thoughts:

_____

_____

_____

_____

_____

_____

I just realized that a tractor trailer horn is a blast. An SUV horn is a honk. A small sedan horn is a beep. And a bike horn is a tinkle. There appears to be a horn hierarchy.

Your Random Thoughts:

_____

_____

_____

_____

_____

_____

When your car runs, it's good. When your nose runs, it's bad. Except for Kleenex®.

Your Random Thoughts:

_____

_____

_____

_____

_____

_____

It's odd to say that someone smokes because it's really the cigarette that smokes.

Your Random Thoughts:

_____

_____

_____

_____

_____

_____

There are backup lights on a car to warn you when it's backing up. But there are no forward lights to warn you when it's coming right at you.

Your Random Thoughts:

_____

_____

_____

_____

_____

_____

Isn't a self-help book really someone else's help?

Your Random Thoughts:

_____

_____

_____

_____

_____

_____

The collars of my shirt are brown. I don't understand how my neck got that dirty.

Your Random Thoughts:

_____

_____

_____

_____

_____

_____

The problem with the English language is that there were no internal controls when it was being developed. For instance, a drinking glass is a glass – unless it has a handle. Then, it's a cup.

Your Random Thoughts:

_____

_____

_____

_____

_____

_____

If my belly button continues to collect lint, I worry that the center of my shirts will eventually disappear.

Your Random Thoughts:

_____

_____

_____

_____

_____

_____

The older I get, the older "old age" gets. That must be the second theory of relativity.

Your Random Thoughts:

_____

_____

_____

_____

_____

_____

There's a bell that dings in my car when I forget to put on my seatbelt. I'd like one of those when my wife forgets to put on her sexy lingerie.

Your Random Thoughts:

_____

_____

_____

_____

_____

_____

A local bakery sells muffin tops. I'm a bottom man myself but there appears to be no market for muffin bottoms.

Your Random Thoughts:

_____

_____

_____

_____

_____

_____

My dog is always happy to see me. Sometimes I say "Bad dog!" in a happy voice just to trick him.

Your Random Thoughts:

_____

_____

_____

_____

_____

_____

The formula for parenting teenagers is 1x = 1y. x = one minute of embarrassing your child; and y = one hour of therapy when your child turns 30.

Your Random Thoughts:

_____

_____

_____

_____

_____

_____

Sometimes I wake up in the morning and don't want to do anything. So, if I don't do anything, then I suppose I have met my goal for the day.

Your Random Thoughts:

_____

_____

_____

_____

_____

_____

The sign in the local coffee shop says, "Fresh Brewed Coffee." This alerts anyone who comes in looking for Stale Instant Coffee.

Your Random Thoughts:

_____

_____

_____

_____

_____

_____

My stereo speakers
don't really speak.
They sound. But if they
were called sounders,
they'd be confused with
that movie about a dog.
Maybe that's where
woofers came from.

Your Random Thoughts:

_____

_____

_____

_____

_____

_____

When I look at a raw oyster, I can't help wonder why someone thought of eating that.

Your Random Thoughts:

_____

_____

_____

_____

_____

_____

I just caught myself thinking about what I was thinking. Technically, that probably doesn't count as a new thought but I wrote it down anyway.

Your Random Thoughts:

_____

_____

_____

_____

_____

_____

The word accident means unintentional so you can't intentionally cause an accident. This is good information to know.

Your Random Thoughts:

_____

_____

_____

_____

_____

_____

IF THE BODY IS 60% WATER, IT SEEMS THAT WE WOULD SLOSH MORE.

Your Random Thoughts:

_____

_____

_____

_____

_____

_____

If I think about
the mechanical
process of walking
while I'm walking,
it messes me up.

Your Random Thoughts:

_____

_____

_____

_____

_____

_____

I'm sure glad humans don't sniff each other's butts like dogs do.

Your Random Thoughts:

_____

_____

_____

_____

_____

_____

55

Reading tricks me into sleeping. No matter how interesting the book is, my eyes will close at some point without my even knowing it.

Your Random Thoughts:

_____

_____

_____

_____

_____

_____

Potato chips are really potato slices. But it would probably be a hassle to change it at this point.

Your Random Thoughts:

_____

_____

_____

_____

_____

_____

As a religious person, I sometimes worry that when I go to heaven, I'll find atheists there. Then, I'll wonder, "Who was right?"

Your Random Thoughts:

_____

_____

_____

_____

_____

_____

If you had shown me bottled water forty years ago, I would have been suspicious.

Your Random Thoughts:

_____

_____

_____

_____

_____

_____

I bite my nails but have no idea why. They're neither nutritious nor tasty. And it's somewhat cannibalistic.

Your Random Thoughts:

_____

_____

_____

_____

_____

_____

I'M TICKLING MYSELF RIGHT NOW. NOTHING.

Your Random Thoughts:

_____

_____

_____

_____

_____

_____

If everyone agreed to sleep at night, we wouldn't need people to work night shifts.

Your Random Thoughts:

_____

_____

_____

_____

_____

_____

My calendar makes me feel stupid. I should know what day it is on my own.

Your Random Thoughts:

_____

_____

_____

_____

_____

_____

I wonder how many people die in plane crashes each year because their seat was not in the upright and locked position.

Your Random Thoughts:

_____

_____

_____

_____

_____

_____

There are farmers who can grow seedless watermelons. That's not farming. That's magic.

Your Random Thoughts:

_____

_____

_____

_____

_____

_____

When I listen to Rock & Roll music, I've never had the urge to rock nor roll.

Your Random Thoughts:

_____

_____

_____

_____

_____

_____

Sometimes I'll leave the gym and go straight to a coffee shop where I'll buy a Giganti Caramel Frozen Coffee Milkshake. Seems to balance out.

Your Random Thoughts:

_____

_____

_____

_____

_____

_____

The cursor on my computer is flashing. It really wants me to know where it is.

Your Random Thoughts:

_____

_____

_____

_____

_____

_____

DNA informed my body to stop growing when I turned 21. My fingernails and hair didn't get the memo.

Your Random Thoughts:

_____

_____

_____

_____

_____

_____

The flight attendant on my plane said that the plane weighed 187,000 pounds. My first thought was, "I shouldn't have eaten that Cinnabon® in the airport."

Your Random Thoughts:

_____

_____

_____

_____

_____

_____

Sometimes I dread Friday because I know that Monday is only three days later.

Your Random Thoughts:

_____

_____

_____

_____

_____

_____

We have even *and* odd numbers. Apparently, someone felt that having uneven numbers was odd.

Your Random Thoughts:

_____

_____

_____

_____

_____

_____

I always heard you weren't supposed to watch the clock. Then, somebody turned clocks into watches. Go figure.

Your Random Thoughts:

_____

_____

_____

_____

_____

_____

If long grass, like long legs, was considered elegant, no one would have to mow their yard.

Your Random Thoughts:

_____

_____

_____

_____

_____

_____

I was just thinking about doing something but that's as far as I've gotten.

Your Random Thoughts:

_____

_____

_____

_____

_____

_____

Daydreaming is my choice. Nightdreaming happens on its own.

Your Random Thoughts:

_____

_____

_____

_____

_____

_____

My skin is waterproof. Not once has rain ever leaked into any of my organs.

Your Random Thoughts:

_____

_____

_____

_____

_____

_____

I shopped many different stores before I bought my computer. I married the only woman I dated in college. That seems backwards.

Your Random Thoughts:

_____

_____

_____

_____

_____

_____

I don't celebrate Columbus Day. I wouldn't know what to cook or what to give as a gift.

Your Random Thoughts:

_____

_____

_____

_____

_____

_____

The word potpourri can refer to anything. That's not very helpful.

Your Random Thoughts:

_____

_____

_____

_____

_____

_____

I realized I've never eaten just one peanut, one kernel of corn, or one pea.

Your Random Thoughts:

_____

_____

_____

_____

_____

_____

My doctor specializes in internal medicine. Seems like, basically, all doctors do.

Your Random Thoughts:

_____

_____

_____

_____

_____

_____

Hair plugs and Chia™ Pets are similar. And both are just wrong.

Your Random Thoughts:

_____

_____

_____

_____

_____

_____

When people get
cosmetic surgery,
I wonder if God
is thinking,
"Go ahead, let's see
what *you* can do."

Your Random Thoughts:

_____

_____

_____

_____

_____

_____

I'd prefer that men cover their chests and women didn't.

Your Random Thoughts:

_____

_____

_____

_____

_____

_____

If our skin and our organs were transparent, we wouldn't need colonoscopies.

Your Random Thoughts:

_____

_____

_____

_____

_____

_____

Philosophers spend time thinking about thinking. That's got to be the ultimate in laziness.

Your Random Thoughts:

_____

_____

_____

_____

_____

_____

I say, "Hello" when I answer the phone but "Who is it?" when I answer the door – even though I can see the person at the door but not the person on the phone.

Your Random Thoughts:

_____

_____

_____

_____

_____

_____

They say a picture's worth a thousand words but I've never tried to come up with them all.

Your Random Thoughts:

_____

_____

_____

_____

_____

_____

Based on the number of them I've seen on the side of the road, cats really don't have nine lives.

Your Random Thoughts:

_____

_____

_____

_____

_____

_____

The phrase mind-body connection seems weird. Because if the mind and body weren't connected, we'd be dead.

Your Random Thoughts:

_____

_____

_____

_____

_____

_____

WHEN I SAY MY FIRST NAME OVER AND OVER, IT STOPS SOUNDING LIKE ME.

Your Random Thoughts:

_____

_____

_____

_____

_____

_____

My joints are a lot more accurate than a meteorologist.

Your Random Thoughts:

_____

_____

_____

_____

_____

_____

I wish I could fly. It would make those last minute trips to the grocery store so much easier.

Your Random Thoughts:

_____

_____

_____

_____

_____

_____

Sometimes I feel like I'm watching myself – in a philosophical sense. But if I tell someone, I'm afraid I'll be placed on medication.

Your Random Thoughts:

_____

_____

_____

_____

_____

_____

Sometimes I move a part of my body and think, "How did I just do that?"

Your Random Thoughts:

_____

_____

_____

_____

_____

_____

I'm an extrovert except when it comes to interacting with other people.

Your Random Thoughts:

_____

_____

_____

_____

_____

_____

Ronald P. Culberson

My doctor always walks into the exam room and says, "Hi, how are you?" I feel like saying, "Funny you should ask."

Your Random Thoughts:

_____

_____

_____

_____

_____

_____

Shouldn't a wristwatch really be called an armclock?

Your Random Thoughts:

_____

_____

_____

_____

_____

_____

The meaning of life is to make life meaningful. Now my brain hurts.

Your Random Thoughts:

_____

_____

_____

_____

_____

_____

Fingernails help us pick up coins. But what the heck do toenails do?

Your Random Thoughts:

_____

_____

_____

_____

_____

_____

Some people want to die quickly with no pain. Some want to linger so they can enjoy time with loved ones. I think I'd rather *not* die.

Your Random Thoughts:

_____

_____

_____

_____

_____

_____

I've never said, "That tastes good. It reminds me of water."

Your Random Thoughts:

_____

_____

_____

_____

_____

_____

103

I'm not sure my wisdom teeth are smarter than the others.

Your Random Thoughts:

_____

_____

_____

_____

_____

_____

If social media keeps you at your computer more, it should be called anti-social media.

Your Random Thoughts:

_____

_____

_____

_____

_____

_____

SOMETIMES, I LOOK AT PARTS OF MY BODY AND WONDER, "WHY DO I GROW HAIR *THERE*?"

Your Random Thoughts:

_____

_____

_____

_____

_____

_____

If someone's last words were grouped together, they would probably form a death sentence.

Your Random Thoughts:

_____

_____

_____

_____

_____

_____

107

Hanky is short for handkerchief but hanky panky is nothing to sneeze at.

Your Random Thoughts:

_____

_____

_____

_____

_____

_____

I just walked into a room and don't remember why. Maybe I should have written down my plans and stuck them in my pocket.

Your Random Thoughts:

_____

_____

_____

_____

_____

_____

Tummy tuck sounds much more appealing than "cut you open, remove stuff, and sew you up tighter than before."

Your Random Thoughts:

_____

_____

_____

_____

_____

_____

It seems that if I indulge in the "hair of the dog that bit me," I'll get bit again.

Your Random Thoughts:

_____

_____

_____

_____

_____

_____

111

We tell time but we read a thermometer. That's good, I guess, since I'm not sure what I'd tell a thermometer anyway.

Your Random Thoughts:

_____

_____

_____

_____

_____

_____

I notice that some people grow up and some people grow out.

Your Random Thoughts:

_____

_____

_____

_____

_____

_____

Just about the time you figure out what's important in life, it ends.

Your Random Thoughts:

_____

_____

_____

_____

_____

_____

I watched a TV show that was rated M for mature audiences. But based on the content, it was really more appropriate for immature audiences.

Your Random Thoughts:

_____

_____

_____

_____

_____

_____

No one will question your taking a sick day if you tell them you have diarrhea.

Your Random Thoughts:

_____

_____

_____

_____

_____

_____

When my barber started using electric clippers *inside* my ears, I knew my youth had passed.

Your Random Thoughts:

_____

_____

_____

_____

_____

_____

If we have influenza, we call it the flu. But if we have pneumonia, we don't call it the pneu.

Your Random Thoughts:

_____

_____

_____

_____

_____

_____

We clap after a good play or a good movie. I never know what to do after reading a good book.

Your Random Thoughts:

_____

_____

_____

_____

_____

_____

Mickey Mouse was the most significant cartoon character ever and yet the phrase "Mickey Mouse" means insignificant.

Your Random Thoughts:

_____

_____

_____

_____

_____

_____

I'm embarrassed to admit it, but I love to say, "Uranus."

Your Random Thoughts:

_____

_____

_____

_____

_____

_____

121

IT'S UNFORTUNATE THAT I CAN'T CALL IN SICK... OF WORK.

Your Random Thoughts:

_____

_____

_____

_____

_____

_____

Ever notice
that when we use
a stopwatch, we
usually say,
"Go."

Your Random Thoughts:

_____

_____

_____

_____

_____

_____

I love math because everything adds up.

Your Random Thoughts:

_____

_____

_____

_____

_____

_____

A dream is like an invitation-only party for our thoughts.

Your Random Thoughts:

_____

_____

_____

_____

_____

_____

125

Capris.
They're not pants.
They're not shorts.
They're not for men.

Your Random Thoughts:

_____

_____

_____

_____

_____

_____

Someone once said, "Today is the first day of the rest of your life." Isn't that obvious?

Your Random Thoughts:

_____

_____

_____

_____

_____

_____

Cookies are named for the process that made them. If the same concept was applied to people, we'd be called bornies.

Your Random Thoughts:

_____

_____

_____

_____

_____

_____

Jesus turned water into wine. The best I can do is turn water into urine.

Your Random Thoughts:

_____

_____

_____

_____

_____

_____

When I misspell a word, it reminds me of a friend whose name was Tuan. The spell check on his computer kept changing his name to Tuna.

Your Random Thoughts:

_____

_____

_____

_____

_____

_____

Wherever I go, there I am. Does that happen to you?

Your Random Thoughts:

_____

_____

_____

_____

_____

_____

Professional entertainers get paid a lot. Trash collectors don't get paid a lot. If trash collectors were more entertaining, maybe they'd get paid more.

Your Random Thoughts:

_____

_____

_____

_____

_____

_____

There are many different ways to cut hair. But everybody gives their yard a crew cut.

Your Random Thoughts:

_____

_____

_____

_____

_____

_____

The older I get, the more faces don't ring a bell.

Your Random Thoughts:

_____

_____

_____

_____

_____

_____

I take one day at a time. I'm not sure it's even possible to take a whole group of days at a time.

Your Random Thoughts:

_____

_____

_____

_____

_____

_____

If I see a penny on the ground, I never pick it up. I've never been in a situation where I said, "If only I had another penny."

Your Random Thoughts:

_____

_____

_____

_____

_____

_____

I don't understand how a good movie can have a bad ending. It's like the director said, "Oh well."

Your Random Thoughts:

_____

_____

_____

_____

_____

_____

RICE IS SHORT BUT IT TAKES A LONG TIME TO COOK.

Your Random Thoughts:

_____

_____

_____

_____

_____

_____

I have a best friend but not a best sibling.

Your Random Thoughts:

_____

_____

_____

_____

_____

_____

I bet the pea and the peanut are related by some sort of contamination of their family tree.

Your Random Thoughts:

_____

_____

_____

_____

_____

_____

Onions make me cry. Jalapeños burn my mouth. Asparagus makes my urine smell bad. Some vegetables are adversarial.

Your Random Thoughts:

_____

_____

_____

_____

_____

_____

141

Baby-sitting should be called baby running-around-the-room-trying-to-keep-up-with-the-brats-ing.

Your Random Thoughts:

_____

_____

_____

_____

_____

_____

I was thinking about giving myself a plaque for having the most plaques in my family.

Your Random Thoughts:

_____

_____

_____

_____

_____

_____

A dozen means twelve. Someone decided that the number 12 was popular enough to give it a nickname.

Your Random Thoughts:

_____

_____

_____

_____

_____

_____

Flying a kite is odd. We would never attach a string to a ball and hold it down a hill.

Your Random Thoughts:

_____

_____

_____

_____

_____

_____

When I go running, the only thought in my head is, "I hate running."

Your Random Thoughts:

_____

_____

_____

_____

_____

_____

People love to correct your grammar and your spelling. They must enjoy catching you with your participle dangling.

Your Random Thoughts:

_____

_____

_____

_____

_____

_____

Ronald P. Culberson

I wonder if anyone has had the bad luck of being injured while trying to *avoid* walking under a ladder.

Your Random Thoughts:

_____

_____

_____

_____

_____

_____

In school I was taught to Stop, Drop, and Roll if I catch on fire. I think we should teach kids to Stop, Turn, and Run to avoid fire in the first place.

Your Random Thoughts:

_____

_____

_____

_____

_____

_____

149

When someone says,
"I don't feel like
myself today," they're
assuming they would
never feel that way.
And yet they do.

Your Random Thoughts:

_____

_____

_____

_____

_____

_____

IT WOULD BE IRONIC IF THE ICING DISPENSER IN A BAKERY GOT CAKED UP.

Your Random Thoughts:

_____

_____

_____

_____

_____

_____

One minute I'm awake and the next minute I'm asleep. I've never really witnessed the process unfold.

Your Random Thoughts:

_____

_____

_____

_____

_____

_____

I enjoy marking items off my to-do list more than doing them.

Your Random Thoughts:

_____

_____

_____

_____

_____

_____

If classical music was considered contemporary when it was being created, that means that one day *Achy Breaky Heart* will be considered classical music.

Your Random Thoughts:

_____

_____

_____

_____

_____

_____

My jeans get tighter the longer I have them. My skin gets looser the longer I have it.

Your Random Thoughts:

_____

_____

_____

_____

_____

_____

I don't think we should celebrate our birthdays. It's not like we had anything to do with it.

Your Random Thoughts:

_____

_____

_____

_____

_____

_____

If we were just willing to round up, we wouldn't need coins.

Your Random Thoughts:

_____

_____

_____

_____

_____

_____

157

The only way to avoid death is to avoid life. But if you avoid life, you'll be dead.

Your Random Thoughts:

_____

_____

_____

_____

_____

_____

Supposedly it is better to give than receive. That's especially true when you give away a really bad gift.

Your Random Thoughts:

_____

_____

_____

_____

_____

_____

I hate it when people tell me to stop complaining.

Your Random Thoughts:

_____

_____

_____

_____

_____

_____

When you think about it, the phrase "he lives next door" really doesn't make much sense.

Your Random Thoughts:

_____

_____

_____

_____

_____

_____

Ronald P. Culberson

If you're challenged by whether the glass is half full or half empty, you could always get a smaller glass.

Your Random Thoughts:

_____

_____

_____

_____

_____

_____

I must confess that when someone starts to tell me a joke and says, "Stop me if you've heard this," I never do. But I probably should.

Your Random Thoughts:

_____

_____

_____

_____

_____

_____

It would be cool if our eyelids had little lights inside. In case we're afraid of the dark.

Your Random Thoughts:

_____

_____

_____

_____

_____

_____

I think extreme sports should really be called you're-going-to-get-hurt sports.

Your Random Thoughts:

_____

_____

_____

_____

_____

_____

Sometimes I like to plan spontaneity. It helps me feel less structured.

Your Random Thoughts:

_____

_____

_____

_____

_____

_____

Was the word "pet" created because you can pet the animals you own? If so, how did fish become pets?

Your Random Thoughts:

_____

_____

_____

_____

_____

_____

I *think* I'm better than I really am at practically everything.

Your Random Thoughts:

_____

_____

_____

_____

_____

_____

It appears that whoever designed women's shoes did not model them after the shape of a woman's foot but instead, the beak of a crow.

Your Random Thoughts:

_____

_____

_____

_____

_____

_____

If you add two
authors to two more
authors you'd get
fourshadowing.

Your Random Thoughts:

_____

_____

_____

_____

_____

_____

If the windows in my house were prescription strength, I wouldn't need my glasses to look outside.

Your Random Thoughts:

_____

_____

_____

_____

_____

_____

171

Someone said we should live each day as if it were our last. If I did that, I'd probably spend the entire day worrying.

Your Random Thoughts:

_____

_____

_____

_____

_____

_____

MY TO-DO LIST WILL NEVER BE TO-DONE.

Your Random Thoughts:

_____

_____

_____

_____

_____

_____

If reality shows are real, then my life is a fantasy.

Your Random Thoughts:

_____

_____

_____

_____

_____

_____

Awe-some means incredible. Aw-ful means miserable. Somebody screwed up on that linguistic assignment.

Your Random Thoughts:

_____

_____

_____

_____

_____

_____

The rains of Noah's flood lasted 40 days. The Jews wondered the desert for 40 years. Women are pregnant for 40 weeks. The work week is 40 hours. God loves the number 40.

Your Random Thoughts:

_____

_____

_____

_____

_____

_____

No matter how many times I've blown my nose, it keeps churning stuff out.

Your Random Thoughts:

_____

_____

_____

_____

_____

_____

177

I wish the older we got, the better we looked. It would make living in a nursing home so much more appealing.

Your Random Thoughts:

_____

_____

_____

_____

_____

_____

I watch spelling bees on television and can't help thinking how smart these kids are. But, they will still get beat up on the playground.

Your Random Thoughts:

_____

_____

_____

_____

_____

_____

I hate to floss.
That felt good to get
that off my chest.

Your Random Thoughts:

_____

_____

_____

_____

_____

_____

IN COLLEGE, I GOT B'S IN MY CLASSES BUT A'S IN MY DISTRACTIONS.

Your Random Thoughts:

_____

_____

_____

_____

_____

_____

181

I wish there were smart bombs for snakes.

Your Random Thoughts:

_____

_____

_____

_____

_____

_____

When I was a kid, I always took a bath. As an adult, sitting in dirty water doesn't really appeal to me.

Your Random Thoughts:

_____

_____

_____

_____

_____

_____

I love caller ID. It's like having a fortune teller inside my phone.

Your Random Thoughts:

_____

_____

_____

_____

_____

_____

What good is a gas gauge when I can drive for miles on E?

Your Random Thoughts:

_____

_____

_____

_____

_____

_____

Whenever I have a deep thought, I feel like I need to wade back in the shallow end where I feel much more comfortable.

Your Random Thoughts:

_____

_____

_____

_____

_____

_____

Swimming is the only recreational sport where if you stop to rest, you die.

Your Random Thoughts:

_____

_____

_____

_____

_____

_____

Ronald P. Culberson

A well-done job is rare. But a rare steak is not well done.

Your Random Thoughts:

_____

_____

_____

_____

_____

_____

It took me a while but I just proved that a watched pot never boils but the water in it does.

Your Random Thoughts:

_____

_____

_____

_____

_____

_____

An apple a day keeps the doctor away. Garlic keeps the vampires away. But nothing seems to keep the mosquitoes off me.

Your Random Thoughts:

_____

_____

_____

_____

_____

_____

I seem to be more focused when self-discipline comes from someone else.

Your Random Thoughts:

_____

_____

_____

_____

_____

_____

Ronald P. Culberson

It feels good to stretch but I have no idea why.

Your Random Thoughts:

_____

_____

_____

_____

_____

_____

I don't think I would want a rice cake for my birthday.

Your Random Thoughts:

_____

_____

_____

_____

_____

_____

Sometimes I wake up in the middle of the night and need to go to the bathroom. But I'm so lazy, I force myself to go back to sleep rather than walk to the bathroom.

Your Random Thoughts:

_____

_____

_____

_____

_____

_____

I love anything crunchy and salty. Well, except for the sand at the beach.

Your Random Thoughts:

_____

_____

_____

_____

_____

_____

CURSE WORDS FEEL REALLY GOOD WHEN USED IN THE RIGHT CIRCUMSTANCES.

Your Random Thoughts:

_____

_____

_____

_____

_____

_____

I take my car in for service every 3,500 miles. But I've gone over 100,000 yards and never changed the oil in my lawnmower.

Your Random Thoughts:

_____

_____

_____

_____

_____

_____

We tip some service professionals but not others. I can't imagine giving my pastor a tip.

Your Random Thoughts:

_____

_____

_____

_____

_____

_____

My doctor has her diploma on the wall. It's as if she's saying, "See, I really am a doctor."

Your Random Thoughts:

_____

_____

_____

_____

_____

_____

Time stops for no one. But it sure slows down for my dentist.

Your Random Thoughts:

_____

_____

_____

_____

_____

_____

When I'm trying to get to the bottom of something, I should probably consult a proctologist.

Your Random Thoughts:

_____

_____

_____

_____

_____

_____

Sometimes I imagine that I'm the only real person in the world and everyone else is just an illusion. That's when I know I need to lay off the caffeine for a while.

Your Random Thoughts:

_____

_____

_____

_____

_____

_____

Occasionally, I'll be minding my own business and all of the sudden, I get a sharp pain somewhere in my body. It's as if little warriors are living in my body and one of them dropped his spear.

Your Random Thoughts:

_____

_____

_____

_____

_____

_____

It wasn't cool but learning "ASDF JKL;" in my high school typing class sure paid off.

Your Random Thoughts:

_____

_____

_____

_____

_____

_____

I got married for better or for worse but I prefer the better.

Your Random Thoughts:

_____

_____

_____

_____

_____

_____

When I'm in the doghouse, I hate it. When the dog is in my house, he loves it.

Your Random Thoughts:

_____

_____

_____

_____

_____

_____

My dental hygienist always reminds me to brush with a soft toothbrush – right after she scrapes my teeth with a metal pick.

Your Random Thoughts:

_____

_____

_____

_____

_____

_____

If there is a purpose for the hair on our heads, which I'm sure in God's infinite wisdom there is, why did I lose mine?

Your Random Thoughts:

_____

_____

_____

_____

_____

_____

I wonder who decided that the sound of a doorbell should be ding-dong instead of ding-ding or dong-dong.

Your Random Thoughts:

_____

_____

_____

_____

_____

_____

209

I've got an interesting thought. Nope. False alarm.

Your Random Thoughts:

_____

_____

_____

_____

_____

_____

It's not Monday I hate, it's *working* on Monday that upsets me.

Your Random Thoughts:

_____

_____

_____

_____

_____

_____

211

Ironically, I have functioned fine for quite some time without ever using the Function Key on my computer.

Your Random Thoughts:

_____

_____

_____

_____

_____

_____

I FIND IT HARD TO MEDITATE BECAUSE OF TRYING TO THINK ABOUT MEDITATING.

Your Random Thoughts:

_____

_____

_____

_____

_____

_____

213

Ronald P. Culberson

I have a craving for so many things. I think it may be the craving I really crave.

Your Random Thoughts:

_____

_____

_____

_____

_____

_____

When you're on an airplane, it's better not to think about the fact that you're inside 187,000 pounds of metal flying at 39,000 feet in the air.

Your Random Thoughts:

_____

_____

_____

_____

.
_____

_____

I used to laugh at
a man in my hometown
that had hair growing
out of his ears. I am
now that man.

Your Random Thoughts:

_____

_____

_____

_____

_____

_____

I sometimes fantasize that my wife is a waitress and when she gets into bed, she'll say, "Hi, I'm Wendy. I'll be taking care of you this evening."

Your Random Thoughts:

_____

_____

_____

_____

_____

_____

217

I wonder if the people who came up with numbers argued over what to call them? I would have enjoyed hearing the debate over eleven vs. onety-one.

Your Random Thoughts:

_____

_____

_____

_____

_____

_____

There are lots of sports on TV. But competitive shuffleboard has never made it to the big time.

Your Random Thoughts:

_____

_____

_____

_____

_____

_____

Toilet paper and paper towels come in a roll. Napkins and facial tissues come in a stack. I don't know who decides these things.

Your Random Thoughts:

_____

_____

_____

_____

_____

_____

The name Band-Aid® does not have anything to do with putting sticky plastic on a laceration.

Your Random Thoughts:

_____

_____

_____

_____

_____

_____

Conveniently, our backs, hips, and knees bend perfectly to fit the shape of a chair.

Your Random Thoughts:

_____

_____

_____

_____

_____

_____

Home is not really where the heart is or else everyone who leaves home would die.

Your Random Thoughts:

_____

_____

_____

_____

_____

_____

The day after your funeral is the first day of the rest of your death.

Your Random Thoughts:

_____

_____

_____

_____

_____

_____

224

God created the dark and the light. But humans created dark rooms and lights. There's no satisfying some people.

Your Random Thoughts:

_____

_____

_____

_____

_____

_____

Ronald P. Culberson

If I needed a gall bladder transplant, just about anybody could be a donor.

Your Random Thoughts:

_____

_____

_____

_____

_____

_____

It's weird. I get through Monday and a week later, it's here again.

Your Random Thoughts:

_____

_____

_____

_____

_____

_____

The slow car in front of me never seems to know that I'm in a hurry.

Your Random Thoughts:

_____

_____

_____

_____

_____

_____

No matter how healthy laughter is, you don't look so good when you do it alone.

Your Random Thoughts:

_____

_____

_____

_____

_____

_____

I don't think athletes would ever eat the food they serve at the concession stands of athletic events.

Your Random Thoughts:

_____

_____

_____

_____

_____

_____

If I had designed the week, I think I would have put Friday after Sunday.

Your Random Thoughts:

_____

_____

_____

_____

_____

_____

When you hear a recording of yourself, you need to realize that you *do* sound like that. All the time.

Your Random Thoughts:

_____

_____

_____

_____

_____

_____

The word cool was popular when I was in high school. Thirty years later, it's popular again. That's cool.

Your Random Thoughts:

_____

_____

_____

_____

_____

_____

233

The word consultant is actually two words. Consult. Ant. People that talk to you and then get into everything.

Your Random Thoughts:

_____

_____

_____

_____

_____

_____

Nobody really wants to go to work. We should call it something else so it would sound more attractive. Maybe lingerie.

Your Random Thoughts:

_____

_____

_____

_____

_____

_____

We should have pre-obituary columns. I'd like to know more about others' accomplishments *before* they die.

Your Random Thoughts:

_____

_____

_____

_____

_____

_____

The vacuum tube at the bank is great. I'd like to have that for my groceries. They could send everything straight from the store to my fridge.

Your Random Thoughts:

_____

_____

_____

_____

_____

_____

Ronald P. Culberson

WHAT KIND OF LEADERSHIP TRAINING DO CHEERLEADERS REALLY HAVE?

Your Random Thoughts:

_____

_____

_____

_____

_____

_____

My dog doesn't have any hobbies. Unless you count his licking himself.

Your Random Thoughts:

_____

_____

_____

_____

_____

_____

I sometimes worry about being accidentally locked up in a psychiatric hospital where the more I tell them I shouldn't be there, the crazier I appear.

Your Random Thoughts:

_____

_____

_____

_____

_____

_____

MY KNEECAP SEEMS TOO LOOSE.

Your Random Thoughts:

_____

_____

_____

_____

_____

_____

Sending a letter is really cheap. I wish airlines could send *me* that inexpensively.

Your Random Thoughts:

_____

_____

_____

_____

_____

_____

When I'm in a moving vehicle, I can always fall asleep. That's problematic when I'm driving.

Your Random Thoughts:

_____

_____

_____

_____

_____

_____

Ronald P. Culberson

When I'm talking to someone who is blind, inevitably, I say, "See what I mean?" I always feel bad about that.

Your Random Thoughts:

_____

_____

_____

_____

_____

_____

It's funny how a dream can be a visionary goal in the daytime but a nightmare at night.

Your Random Thoughts:

_____

_____

_____

_____

_____

_____

245

Ronald P. Culberson

I get hungry right around mealtimes. That's convenient.

Your Random Thoughts:

_____

_____

_____

_____

_____

_____

If time flies when *I'm* having fun, shouldn't it be flying for everyone else too?

Your Random Thoughts:

_____

_____

_____

_____

_____

_____

If someone says, "When all's said and done," they're never done with what's being said.

Your Random Thoughts:

_____

_____

_____

_____

_____

_____

I realized that I have something in common with the Post Office. I *am* a U.S. male.

Your Random Thoughts:

_____

_____

_____

_____

_____

_____

Surgeons are always removing things. But you never see a mechanic take something out of your car and say, "You don't really need this."

Your Random Thoughts:

_____

_____

_____

_____

_____

_____

If men gave up TV, I bet their thumbs would gain weight.

Your Random Thoughts:

_____

_____

_____

_____

_____

_____

Laughter gives you a second wind. Sometimes it causes the first wind.

Your Random Thoughts:

_____

_____

_____

_____

_____

_____

I think doctors keep us in the waiting room so long because they hope we'll get better on our own.

Your Random Thoughts:

_____

_____

_____

_____

_____

_____

I went to a conference where they offered mini massages. I'd never had my mini massaged.

Your Random Thoughts:

_____

_____

_____

_____

_____

_____

I'm thinking of hooking my GPS up to caller ID. Then, I could find the telemarketers.

Your Random Thoughts:

_____

_____

_____

_____

_____

_____

When my wife asks me if a dress makes her look fat, I always answer truthfully. "No that dress doesn't make you look fat. That sleeve of Girl Scout cookies you ate last night makes you look fat."

Your Random Thoughts:

_____

_____

_____

_____

_____

_____

Toothaches, headaches, earaches, and stomachaches are very common. Noseaches, eyebrowaches, and lipaches are not as common in the aching community.

Your Random Thoughts:

_____

_____

_____

_____

_____

_____

When it comes to stamps
or envelopes, we lick
indiscriminately. And we
do not hesitate to handle a
letter that someone else has
licked. That's a lot of saliva
being passed around.

Your Random Thoughts:

_____

_____

_____

_____

_____

_____

Leather shoes are made from dead cows. The cow may be gone but the sole is still there.

Your Random Thoughts:

_____

_____

_____

_____

_____

_____

I will walk nearly two miles every morning. And yet I ask my son to bring me something from a refrigerator that's 20 feet away.

Your Random Thoughts:

_____

_____

_____

_____

_____

_____

People would be much more fun to watch if their knees bent in both directions.

Your Random Thoughts:

_____

_____

_____

_____

_____

_____

If I get lost, I wonder if I could use Google Earth to find me.

Your Random Thoughts:

_____

_____

_____

_____

_____

_____

I'd love to hear this
at an athletic event:
"Two, four, six, eight,
who do we appreciate?
Even numbers!"

Your Random Thoughts:

_____

_____

_____

_____

_____

_____

If an entertainer asked me to give him a hand, I wouldn't know if he needed help or wanted applause.

Your Random Thoughts:

_____

_____

_____

_____

_____

_____

Tennessee is known as the Volunteer State. But I know of at least six people who get paid there.

Your Random Thoughts:

_____

_____

_____

_____

_____

_____

If you watch a scary video with the music off, it's not that scary. If you watch it with the TV off, it's not scary at all.

Your Random Thoughts:

_____

_____

_____

_____

_____

_____

Sometimes, I imagine how hard it would be to explain Facebook® to a caveman.

Your Random Thoughts:

_____

_____

_____

_____

_____

_____

267

It's odd that in American football, putting a foot on the ball is not nearly as common as putting a hand on the ball.

Your Random Thoughts:

_____

_____

_____

_____

_____

_____

I HAVE A CHEAP BOOKSHELF THAT DEVELOPED VENEERIAL DISEASE.

Your Random Thoughts:

_____

_____

_____

_____

_____

_____

Ronald P. Culberson

I don't think my dog participates in the dog days of summer.

Your Random Thoughts:

_____

_____

_____

_____

_____

_____

270

I wonder if the guy who invented doors came from a long line of builders who died inside the rooms they had built.

Your Random Thoughts:

_____

_____

_____

_____

_____

_____

Here's a coincidence.
I'm thinking of this
sentence and now,
so are you.

Your Random Thoughts:

_____

_____

_____

_____

_____

_____

The guy who said, "What goes up must come down," was not telling us anything we don't already know. But he sure gets quoted a lot.

Your Random Thoughts:

_____

_____

_____

_____

_____

_____

No matter how unique the color of your new car is, you will see hundreds of cars in the same color on the way home from the dealer.

Your Random Thoughts:

_____

_____

_____

_____

_____

_____

TWO WRONGS DON'T MAKE A RIGHT BUT THREE LEFT TURNS DO.

Your Random Thoughts:

_____

_____

_____

_____

_____

_____

275

Ronald P. Culberson

Looking before you leap is not that critical if you don't leap much.

Your Random Thoughts:

_____

_____

_____

_____

_____

_____

Every time I cross a street,
I look left, then right,
and then left again. As
if someone was waiting
until I turned my head
to drive towards me.

Your Random Thoughts:

_____

_____

_____

_____

_____

_____

Ronald P. Culberson

Instead of using the doorbell, some people prefer to knock. I guess they haven't embraced the rapid advance of technology.

Your Random Thoughts:

_____

_____

_____

_____

_____

_____

Why do we wear a pair of pants but a single shirt when they both cover two limbs?

Your Random Thoughts:

_____

_____

_____

_____

_____

_____

Whenever I wave to someone and then discover I don't know them after all, I pretend I was waving to someone behind them. It never works.

Your Random Thoughts:

_____

_____

_____

_____

_____

_____

We encourage people to chug a beer as a way to get them drunk faster. We'd never encourage someone to chug a soda as a way to get them diabetes faster.

Your Random Thoughts:

_____

_____

_____

_____

_____

_____

We always compare dog years to people years. But I never hear someone say, "In cow years, he's seventy."

Your Random Thoughts:

_____

_____

_____

_____

_____

_____

There are certain jobs where it would be odd to whistle while you work. Working at a funeral home, for example.

Your Random Thoughts:

_____

_____

_____

_____

_____

_____

When I watch a movie in surround sound, every once in a while, I hear something behind me that startles me.

Your Random Thoughts:

_____

_____

_____

_____

_____

_____

When I gamble, I'm always pretty sure the next bet will be the winner. Reminds me of college when I thought the next test score was going to be an A.

Your Random Thoughts:

_____

_____

_____

_____

_____

_____

Ronald P. Culberson

MY WIFE GOES SHOPPING. I GO GETTING.

Your Random Thoughts:

_____

_____

_____

_____

_____

_____

When someone knocks at the door and my dog barks, I wonder if he's barking at the threat of an intruder or simply informing us, "HEY, THERE'S SOMEBODY AT THE DOOR. THERE'S SOMEBODY AT THE DOOR."

Your Random Thoughts:

_____

_____

_____

_____

_____

_____

287

Ronald P. Culberson

The word "underpants" is funny no matter how it's used.

Your Random Thoughts:

_____

_____

_____

_____

_____

_____

When I got my driver's license photo retaken, I tried to look like I was about to throw up. That way, when I get pulled over and the cop looks at my license, it will look like I feel.

Your Random Thoughts:

_____

_____

_____

_____

_____

_____

Even though I say a book is so good I can't put it down, eventually, I put it down. So, in a way, I guess it's not really *that* good.

Your Random Thoughts:

_____

_____

_____

_____

_____

_____

When someone is called "big boned," I always wonder what accounts for the fat on top of the bones.

Your Random Thoughts:

_____

_____

_____

_____

_____

_____

Let's be honest. Call-ahead seating is really a last-minute reservation.

Your Random Thoughts:

_____

_____

_____

_____

_____

_____

I have a middle name and an appendix. I rarely use either.

Your Random Thoughts:

_____

_____

_____

_____

_____

_____

I imagine that a hair tattoo might make my bald spot less noticeable.

Your Random Thoughts:

_____

_____

_____

_____

_____

_____

There is a new airport x-ray machine that can see through your clothes. But you still have to empty your pockets. What kind of advance is this? It can see your underwear but not a knife in your pocket.

Your Random Thoughts:

_____

_____

_____

_____

_____

_____

Ronald P. Culberson

I've never found a pair of jeans that actually fit me. I must be denim impaired.

Your Random Thoughts:

_____

_____

_____

_____

_____

_____

If the DMV is responsible for organ donations, I sure hope I never need one. Can you imagine the line?

Your Random Thoughts:

_____

_____

_____

_____

_____

_____

Ronald P. Culberson

All-you-can-eat buffets are really all-you-want-to-eat buffets. Otherwise, there would be a lot of vomiting.

Your Random Thoughts:

_____

_____

_____

_____

_____

_____

298

With technology progressing at such a rapid rate, one day, babies may be born cordlessly.

Your Random Thoughts:

_____

_____

_____

_____

_____

_____

The next time I take a vision test, I'm going to say, "E, uh, I, uh, E, I, O. That will be funny. To me.

Your Random Thoughts:

_____

_____

_____

_____

_____

_____

Since the thought of caffeine gets me excited, you'd think I wouldn't need to drink it.

Your Random Thoughts:

_____

_____

_____

_____

_____

_____

Whenever I tell someone I have a motorcycle, they always tell me someone they know that died on a motorcycle. That's not right. You wouldn't tell a fat person that you knew someone who ate so much, they exploded.

Your Random Thoughts:

_____

_____

_____

_____

_____

_____

A HEAVY RAIN
DOES NOT RESEMBLE
CATS AND DOGS.

Your Random Thoughts:

_____

_____

_____

_____

_____

_____

When the security guard at the airport checks my I.D., I'm always afraid that he's thinking, "Nope. Neither one of you looks good."

Your Random Thoughts:

_____

_____

_____

_____

_____

_____

An appetizer should stimulate your appetite but in reality, it fills you up. If you want to stimulate someone's appetite, you should show them the appetizer but not let them eat it.

Your Random Thoughts:

_____

_____

_____

_____

_____

_____

When people say,
"in other words,"
I can't help wondering
why they didn't use
the other words to
begin with.

Your Random Thoughts:

_____

_____

_____

_____

_____

_____

Sometimes I talk back to an answering machine when the person pretends to be answering the phone. I feel so stupid, I'd like to drive to their house and smack them.

Your Random Thoughts:

_____

_____

_____

_____

_____

_____

I imagine a greeting card for Independence Day that would look like this: "Thinking of you as I celebrate our dominance over England."

Your Random Thoughts:

_____

_____

_____

_____

_____

_____

It sucks to get old. But I guess it's worse to stop getting old.

Your Random Thoughts:

_____

_____

_____

_____

_____

_____

A friend introduced his wife as his "first wife." If I were her, I'd introduce myself as his soon-to-be widow.

Your Random Thoughts:

_____

_____

_____

_____

_____

_____

In Bermuda, my father's black socks and shorts would be fashionable.

Your Random Thoughts:

_____

_____

_____

_____

_____

_____

I've made a million faces in my life and not one of them froze.

Your Random Thoughts:

_____

_____

_____

_____

_____

_____

My parents used to remind me to use my turn signal when I was learning to drive. Ironically, I now have to remind them to turn theirs off.

Your Random Thoughts:

_____

_____

_____

_____

_____

_____

**They say that the mind
is the first thing to go.
Actually I think the bowels
are the first thing to go
and when your mind goes,
you just forgot that your
bowels went first.**

Your Random Thoughts:

_____

_____

_____

_____

_____

_____

Sometimes my brain gets so flustered, I call my children by the wrong name. What's worse, sometimes I use my dog's name.

Your Random Thoughts:

_____

_____

_____

_____

_____

_____

I'm not sure why they're called "business cards." It's not like I have a "personal card" that has my name and home address on it.

Your Random Thoughts:

_____

_____

_____

_____

_____

_____

If hotels gave you a larger bar of soap, they wouldn't have to put a new little one in your room every day.

Your Random Thoughts:

_____

_____

_____

_____

_____

_____

My driveway is not very narrow. But apparently it's too narrow for the newspaper delivery person to pull off a direct hit.

Your Random Thoughts:

_____

_____

_____

_____

_____

_____

I think there is a law of physics that says: If you are standing in a customer service line, the line next to you will move at a speed that is inversely proportional to the greater number of people in it.

Your Random Thoughts:

_____

_____

_____

_____

_____

_____

Ronald P. Culberson

EVERY TIME
I SEE TWINS,
I'M BOTH AMAZED
AND UNSETTLED.

Your Random Thoughts:

_____

_____

_____

_____

_____

_____

The Lay-Z-Boy® recliner should really be called the Lay-Z-Man recliner.

Your Random Thoughts:

_____

_____

_____

_____

_____

_____

Ronald P. Culberson

Do you think that when we refer to it as a "stop light," the yellow and green lights feel neglected?

Your Random Thoughts:

_____

_____

_____

_____

_____

_____

I can't respect the diagnosis of Restless Leg Syndrome any more than I could respect the diagnosis of Buttocks Fidget Syndrome.

Your Random Thoughts:

_____

_____

_____

_____

_____

_____

As a man, I can squeeze a lot of sympathy mileage out of a mild case of the flu.

Your Random Thoughts:

_____

_____

_____

_____

_____

_____

When someone says, "I'd hate to meet him in a dark alley," I can't help wondering why they would be in a dark alley to begin with?

Your Random Thoughts:

_____

_____

_____

_____

_____

_____

If a tree falls in the forest and no one is there to hear it, it probably doesn't matter. If a tree falls on me in a forest and I didn't hear it, it probably mattered.

Your Random Thoughts:

_____

_____

_____

_____

_____

_____

The five-second rule has saved a lot of food from certain discardment.

Your Random Thoughts:

_____

_____

_____

_____

_____

_____

If a man threatened to kill Cap'n Crunch®, I guess he'd be a cereal killer.

Your Random Thoughts:

_____

_____

_____

_____

_____

_____

I'm teaching the grass in my yard to smoke. I'm hoping it will stunt its growth.

Your Random Thoughts:

_____

_____

_____

_____

_____

_____

Ronald P. Culberson

We have ten toes and ten fingers because they apparently prefer the metric system?

Your Random Thoughts:

_____

_____

_____

_____

_____

_____

Man cannot live by bread alone. I guess that's why coffee, chocolate, and sex round out the quartet.

Your Random Thoughts:

_____

_____

_____

_____

_____

_____

Sometimes I wish my life had a Ctrl-Alt-Del button so that I could reboot to a previous state.

Your Random Thoughts:

_____

_____

_____

_____

_____

_____

A maid came to my hotel room and asked me if I wanted "turn down" service. I've been turned down enough in my life so I said, "No, thank you."

Your Random Thoughts:

_____

_____

_____

_____

_____

_____

There are a few random hairs in between my eyebrows. It's as if they weren't watching where they were growing.

Your Random Thoughts:

_____

_____

_____

_____

_____

_____

It seems that service animals are just another form of slavery.

Your Random Thoughts:

_____

_____

_____

_____

_____

_____

Ronald P. Culberson

If you want to guarantee good dreams at night, fall asleep watching reruns of *Baywatch*.

Your Random Thoughts:

_____

_____

_____

_____

_____

_____

The only logic I can find to the shelving system in a grocery store is that none of the four items on my list are anywhere near each other.

Your Random Thoughts:

_____

_____

_____

_____

_____

_____

Similar to the Nile, I'm not sure where my fingernails begin.

Your Random Thoughts:

_____

_____

_____

_____

_____

_____

If we weren't supposed to put our fingers in our ear, then why do they fit so perfectly?

Your Random Thoughts:

_____

_____

_____

_____

_____

_____

When someone uses a word I don't recognize, I nod my head hoping the rest of what they say isn't dependent on knowing it.

Your Random Thoughts:

_____

_____

_____

_____

_____

_____

NOTHING GOOD EVER HAPPENS BEFORE, "UH OH."

Your Random Thoughts:

_____

_____

_____

_____

_____

_____

Ronald P. Culberson

If kidding means to joke around, then being serious should be called adulting.

Your Random Thoughts:

_____

_____

_____

_____

_____

_____

I don't think I've ever kept an eye out for anyone.

Your Random Thoughts:

_____

_____

_____

_____

_____

_____

Ronald P. Culberson

I would have rather been stoned in the '60's than stoned in the Bible.

Your Random Thoughts:

_____

_____

_____

_____

_____

_____

Whenever I say the words movie, walkie talkie, or panty, I feel silly.

Your Random Thoughts:

_____

_____

_____

_____

_____

_____

345

Rather than saying "I don't care," sometimes I'll say, "I couldn't care less" as if the care scale extends below zero.

Your Random Thoughts:

_____

_____

_____

_____

_____

_____

The sound of opera and the sound of a dentist drill have the same effect on me.

Your Random Thoughts:

_____

_____

_____

_____

_____

_____

The Lost and Found Department is really the Found Department. The lost stuff is, well, still lost.

Your Random Thoughts:

_____

_____

_____

_____

_____

_____

I've never once put my briefs in my brief case. Probably because I wear boxers.

Your Random Thoughts:

_____

_____

_____

_____

_____

_____

We used to refer to fraternities as frats. But I don't recall ever referring to sororities as sors.

Your Random Thoughts:

_____

_____

_____

_____

_____

_____

As a child, I looked forward to cheap prizes inside boxes of cereal. I still do.

Your Random Thoughts:

_____

_____

_____

_____

_____

_____

The ultimate thrill ride is that moment when you're dropping off to sleep and you think you're falling. It's pure imaginary adrenaline.

Your Random Thoughts:

_____

_____

_____

_____

_____

_____

Dogs can hear high pitch sounds. Cats can hear can openers. Wives can hear pages turning in the Victoria's Secret® catalog.

Your Random Thoughts:

_____

_____

_____

_____

_____

_____

Sometimes I'm in the bathroom and I grapple with knowing the optimum number of toilet paper squares that should be used for good hygiene. I think it may be five.

Your Random Thoughts:

_____

_____

_____

_____

_____

_____

(Just couldn't think of anything today.)

Your Random Thoughts:

_____

_____

_____

_____

_____

_____

Ronald P. Culberson

I finally figured out how to deal with my dental hygienist. I'll tell her that I'm a recreational flosser.

Your Random Thoughts:

_____

_____

_____

_____

_____

_____

MY EARS COME IN VERY HANDY WHEN I'M WEARING GLASSES.

Your Random Thoughts:

_____

_____

_____

_____

_____

_____

There are very few disappointments greater than realizing, while in the shower, that the hot water heater is not working.

Your Random Thoughts:

_____

_____

_____

_____

_____

_____

Unlike deaths which come in three's, home repairs seem to come a dozen at a time.

Your Random Thoughts:

_____

_____

_____

_____

_____

_____

Ronald P. Culberson

Even though cumin and cinnamon both start with a "c" and both have a similar appearance, they do *not* taste the same on oatmeal.

Your Random Thoughts:

_____

_____

_____

_____

_____

_____

I just realized you could read ahead in this book and it wouldn't spoil the ending.

Your Random Thoughts:

_____

_____

_____

_____

_____

_____

I wish I had a hindsight mirror. At the bottom, in small print, it would probably say, "Decisions in mirror are easier than they appeared."

Your Random Thoughts:

_____

_____

_____

_____

_____

_____

MY SIDEBURNS AREN'T EVEN HOT.

Your Random Thoughts:

_____

_____

_____

_____

_____

_____

When a cop asks me if I know why he pulled me over, just for fun, I'd like to say, "No, do you know what I have in the trunk?" Probably not a good idea.

Your Random Thoughts:

_____

_____

_____

_____

_____

_____

All is said and done.

Your Random Thoughts:

_____

_____

_____

_____

_____

_____

The following pages were necessary
to achieve the proper number of pages
for economical printing resulting in bonus
room for your random thoughts.
Enjoy.

Your Random Thoughts Overflow:

_____

_____

_____

_____

_____

_____

_____

_____

_____

_____

_____

_____

_____

_____

_____

_____

Random Thoughts Not Previously Thought:

_____

_____

_____

_____

_____

_____

_____

_____

_____

_____

_____

_____

_____

_____

Actual Random Thoughts Incorrectly Identified as Orderly and Predictable Thoughts:

_____

_____

_____

_____

_____

_____

_____

_____

_____

_____

_____

_____

_____

_____